Tawheed for Kids
Saudi Arabia Curriculum

Book 1

© Saudi Arabia Curriculum, 2020

Tawheed for Kids Class 1. /
- Al Madinah Al Munawwarah , 2020
63p ; ..cm
ISBN: 978-603-03-3708-8
1- Tauhid 2- Islamic theology I-Title
240 dc 1441/6987
L.D. no. 1441/6987
ISBN: 978-603-03-3708-8

TAWHEED FOR KIDS
SAUDI ARABIA CURRICULUM

BOOK 1

Table of contents

بسم الله الرحمن الرحيم

Tawheed (التوحيد)

Tawheed is to single out Allah in all types of worship. So whatever is considered to be worship, which is to do an act which is pleasing to Allah in order to get closer to Allah and follow the path that Allah has commanded His slaves to follow. So the Muslim does every action in order to please his Creator, his Sustainer, and his Owner who is Allah alone. This is the intention of doing all good deeds.

Tawheed is of three different types

First is the **Islam** of Lordship this in Arabic is called Ar-Ruboobiyya which comes from the word Rabb (Lord). Our Lord, Allah the Most High is our Creator, our Sustainer, our Provider, and our Owner.

The second type of **Islam** is the **Islam** of worship. Once we have recognized and come to know that Allah is our Lord then we should truly believe that only Allah has the right to be worshipped in truth. And no one other than Allah deserves to be worshipped since only Allah alone is our true Lord. In Arabic the **Islam** of Worship is called **Tawheed Al-Uloohiyya.**

The third type of **Islam** is the **Islam** of the names and attributes of Allah the Most High. In Arabic it is called **Islam "Al-Asma-was-Sifaat"** Allah has many names and many attributes. Allah is not like anything. Allah is not like any of the creation. Allah is the Greatest. In the Noble Quran Allah describes Himself:

Allah ﷻ is the **All-Hearing.**

Allah ﷻ **is the All-Seeing**

Allah ﷻ **is the Most Merciful.**

The names and attributes of Allah the Most High are perfect and complete. The attributes of the creation are imperfect. So, for example, Allah can see everything and hear everything at any time and place. But a human can only see what is in front of him and hear that which is close to him.

So now we will explain the different types of Tawheed so that a Muslim can know who Allah is and how to worship Him. Allah is above the sky, Allah is above the Arsh (the throne) in a manner that befits His Majesty. This is a very important belief of the Muslim to know "where is Allah?" The meaning of "Allah is with you" is that Allah has complete knowledge of you and that Allah will aid the Muslim who calls upon Him.

Learn about
Islam

Islam is my religion.

Islam means:

Islam is to submit to the will of **Allah** through Tawheed, then fully complying to **Allah** with obedience, and freeing one from Shirk and its people.

The word '**Islam**' indicates submission to **Allah** (Exalted be He), humbling oneself to Him, worshipping Him, and obeying His commands therefore seeking the pleasure of **Allah**, who is your Lord. The essence of Tawheed, is to be completely devoted and submitted to **Allah** (Exalted be He). The true Muslim, who understands Tawheed, is the one who submits himself to **Allah**, devotes his deeds solely to Him, and directs his heart to **Allah** (Exalted be He) in secret and open, in fear and hope, in sayings, deeds, and in everything.

The proof is the saying of **Allah**, the Most Merciful:

$$إِنَّ الدِّينَ عِندَ اللَّهِ الْإِسْلَامُ$$

Indeed the religion with **Allah** is **Islam**. (Surah Aali Imran: 19)

Here **Allah**, the Most High is informing us that the only religion He will accept is **Islam**.

Complete the following sentences:

Islam is:

To Submit your will to the will of **Allah** with T _ _ _ _ _ d

To fully comply with the commands of Allah.

Complete o _ _ _ _ _ n c e.

The Muslim should free himself from Shirk (making partners with Allah) and the people of S _ _ _ k.

The only accepted religion by **Allah** is

_____

- The religion of truth: **Islam**

- **Islam** is the only religion of truth

- Every other religion other than **Islam** is false.

- I do not want a religion other than **Islam**. **Islam** is my religion.

- The proof is the saying of Allah, the Truthful one:

وَمَن يَبْتَغِ غَيْرَ الْإِسْلَام دِينًا فَلَن يُقْبَلَ مِنْهُ
وَهُوَ فِي الآخِرَةِ مِنَ الْخَاسِرِينَ

And whoever desires a religion other than **Islam**, it will never be accepted

from him, and he will be among the losers in the Hereafter.[Surah Ali'Imran:85]

Important Dua:

'"Oh turner of the hearts' [Allah], keep my heart firm upon your religion (Islam)" Narrated by Ahmed and Tirmidhi.

The heart needs to be kept alive by the remembrance of **Allah**, by reciting the Quran and by making Zikr. The dead heart is the one which does not remember **Allah**.

The Pillars of
Islam

Islam is built upon 5 pillars.

The proof is the saying of the Prophet ﷺ:

'Islam is built upon five [pillars]: testifying that there is none worthy of worship except **Allah** and that **Muhammad** is the Messenger of **Allah**, establishing the prayers, giving zakat, making the pilgrimage to the House and fasting the month of Ramadan.' (Bukhari & Muslim).

Complete the following sentences:

The pillars of **Islam** are:

1. To testify that none has the right to be worshipped in truth except **Allah** and **Muhammad** is the Messenger of Allah.

2. Establishing the _____

3. Giving charity which is called _____

4. Making the pilgrimage to the House of Allah, in the city of Makkah al-Mukarramah, which is called _____

5. Fasting in the month of

 The Muslim should take care of these pillars, firstly have knowledge of them and then perform the actions. If the pillars are strong then Emaan is also strong.

Learn about the Messenger of Allah ﷺ

My Prophet is Muhammad bin Abdullah bin Abdul Mutallib bin Hashim, Hashim from the tribe of Al-Quraish, who is from the Arabs.

Allah ﷻ sent our Prophet Muhammad ﷺ to all of mankind to call them to Islam, the worship of Allah.

The Proof is the saying of Allah:

قُلْ يَا أَيُّهَا النَّاسُ إِنِّي رَسُولُ اللَّهِ إِلَيْكُمْ جَمِيعًا

Say, [O Muhammad], "O mankind, indeed I am the Messenger of Allah to you all.[Surah Al'Araf:158]

Allah revealed the Quran onto our Prophet Muhammad ﷺ. The Angel Jibraeel heard the Quran which is the speech of Allah and then revealed it to the Prophet ﷺ.

The Proof is the saying of **Allah**:

إِنَّا نَحْنُ نَزَّلْنَا عَلَيْكَ الْقُرْآنَ تَنْزِيلًا

Indeed, it is We who have sent down to you, [O Muhammad], the Qur'an in stages. [Surah Al-Insan: 23]

Connect from Table A to what is correct from Table B

A	B
Our Prophet Muhammad bin	All of mankind
Allah sent Muhammad ﷺ to	The Noble Quran
Allah revealed onto our Prophet ﷺ	Abdullah bin Abdul Mutallib

Muhammad is the slave of Allah and His Messenger

My Prophet ﷺ is a slave of Allah from the slaves of Allah

The Proof is the saying of Allah ﷻ:

الْحَمْدُ لِلّٰهِ الَّذِي أَنْزَلَ عَلَى عَبْدِهِ الْكِتَابَ

All praise is due to Allah the one who sent down the Book (Quran) onto His slave. [Surah Al-Kahf: 1]

My Prophet **Muhammad** ﷺ is the best of mankind.

My Prophet **Muhammad** ﷺ is the Last of the Messengers sent by **Allah** ﷻ.

The Proof is the saying of **Allah**:

وَلَكِن رَّسُولَ اللّٰهِ وَخَاتَمَ النَّبِيِّينَ

But [he is] the Messenger of Allah

and last of the prophets. [Surah Al-Ahzab: 40]

I say the following Zikr, three times every morning and evening:

رَضِيتُ بِاللهِ رَيًّا ، وَبِالْإِسْلَامِ دِينًا ، وَبِمُحَمَّدٍ رَسُولًا

I am pleased that Allah is the Lord; Islam is the religion and Muhammad in the Messenger.

It is also recommended to say this when the Muezzin (the one who calls the Adhan) says

أشهد أن لا إله إلا الله وأشهد أن محمدًا رسول الله

Which is the correct answer?

Muhammad ﷺ is the

First Messenger ☐   Last Messenger ☐

Who is the best of mankind? .....

....

I love the Messenger of Allah ﷺ

I love my Prophet **Muhammad** ﷺ

I believe in the call of **Muhammad** ﷺ - everything he informed us through the Quran and the Sunnah is totally true.

I obey the Prophet ﷺ and do not disobey him.

Whoever obeys the Prophet ﷺ will enter paradise.

Allah the Most High said:

وَمَن يُطِعِ اللَّهَ وَرَسُولَهُ يُدْخِلْهُ جَنَّاتٍ تَجْرِي
مِن تَحْتَهَا الْأَنْهَارُ خَالِدِينَ فِيهَا وَذَلِكَ
الْفَوْزُ الْعَظِيمُ

Whoever obeys Allah and His Messenger will be admitted by Him to gardens [in Paradise] under which rivers flow, living there forever; and that is a great success. [Surah Al-Nisa: 13]

When the name of the Prophet Muhammad ﷺ is mentioned we say:

This is a Dua that a person recites to ask Allah the Most High to have mercy, to forgive, to aid the Deen of **Muhammad** ﷺ, to mention and praise **Muhammad** ﷺ in front of the angels in the Heavens.

Who is your Prophet?

My Prophet is **Muhammad** ﷺ.

Who Created Us?

Allah is the one who created me and all of the mankind.

Allah is the one who created the skies and the earth. The world has many countries and Islam has spread to almost every country in the world.

Every year Muslims come from the different countries to perform Hajj at Makkah Al-Mukaramah, Saudi Arabia.

Allah is the one who created the sun.

Allah is the one who created the moon.

Allah is the one who created the birds and the animals.

Allah is the greatest.

The proof is the saying of Allah ﷻ

اللَّهُ خَالِقُ كُلِّ شَيْءٍ

"Allah is the creator of everything."

I am a Muslim who submits to what **Allah** wishes and therefore I obey **Allah**, the one who created me. I love **Allah** more than anything else, I fear **Allah** and I have Tawakkal (dependence, hope) in **Allah**.

Allah is the one who provides the food and the air I breathe.

Allah is the one who provides for all of mankind.

Allah is the one who sends the rain from the sky.

Allah said "And we sent from the Sky

pure water" [Surah Al-Furqan: 48]

وَأَنزَلْنَا مِنَ السَّمَاءِ مَاءً طَهُورًا

Allah is the one who makes the plants and the trees grow.

If there is no water, then the earth becomes barren and it is too poor to produce crops and you can't live on it. Nothing will grow on dead land. So we should thank Allah the Most Merciful for sending down the rain, which is a mercy for us.

When it rains the earth becomes full of life and it produces trees, fruits and vegetables.

When it rains we say:

And after the rain we say

اللهم صيبا نافعا

O Allah make the rain beneficial

It rained on us due to the blessings of **Allah** and His Mercy.

It rains with the command of **Allah** alone.

All blessings are from Allah ﷻ alone so therefore we need to be grateful to Allah at all times.

Allah ﷻ is the one who has blessed us so that we can hear and see.

Allah is the one who has blessed us with food and drink.

The Blessings of Allah ﷻ are too many to count, they are countless.

Allah the Most High said:

وَإِن تَعُدُّوا نِعْمَةَ اللّهِ لَا تُحْصُوهَا

"And if you were to count the blessings of Allah then you are never able to count them."[Surah An-Nahl: 18]

So I thank **Allah** for all of the blessings He has given me.

After we eat and drink then we say

I love Allah!!

I love **Allah** because He is the one who guided me to **Islam**.

I love **Allah** because He is the one who created me.

I love **Allah** because He is the one who provided for me.

I love **Allah** because He is the one who blessed me.

Allah the Most High said in the Quran [Surah Al-Baqarah: 165]:

وَالَّذِينَ آمَنُوا أَشَدُّ حُبًّا لِلَّهِ

"But those who believe in Allah then they love Allah a lot [more than anything else]."

I worship **Allah** alone.

I make Dua to **Allah** alone.

I pray for the sake of Allah alone.

Allah created all of the creation, the mankind and Jinn to worship **Allah** alone.

Allah said:

$$وَمَا خَلَقْتُ الْجِنَّ وَالْإِنسَ إِلَّا لِيَعْبُدُونِ$$

"I did not create the Jinn or Mankind except that they worship Me alone." [Surah Adh-Dhaariyat:56]

So **Allah** created all of Mankind for one reason only. That is that they worship Allah in the same way that **Allah** taught the Prophet Muhammad ﷺ.

Allah created the humans

Allah created the Sun and the Moon

Allah created the animals.

Allah is the one who sends down the rain from the sky.

Allah created everything that exists.

Allah said in the Noble Quran:

$$اللَّهُ خَالِقُ كُلِّ شَيْءٍ$$

"**Allah** is the creator of everything."
[Surah Az-Zumar: 62]

Why did Allah create us?

Everything in life has a purpose, a reason why it is created. The only reason why **Allah** ﷻ created human beings is that they worship Him alone.

Allah said in the

Quran:

وَمَا خَلَقْتُ الْجِنَّ وَالْإِنسَ إِلَّا لِيَعْبُدُونِ

"I did not create the Jinn or Mankind except that they worship Me alone."[Surah Adh-Dhaariyat: 56]

A Muslim should fear **Allah** and do not disobey Allah.

Allah created me so that I may worship **Allah** alone, so I pray and I fast for the sake of **Allah** alone. I give charity and I obey my parents.

I love **Allah** and I obey **Allah** because **Allah** created me and provided for me and made me one of the Muslims.

What is Worship?

Worship is called Ibaadah in Arabic.

Ibaadah is what Allah loves from the sayings and actions of a person.

There are many types of worship such as praying, fasting, reading the Quran, obeying the parents, helping the neighbour, giving charity and also not to lie.

Islam is the religion of truth, the only religion accepted by **Allah**.

Islam is to submit to **Allah** with **Tawheed** and to have total obedience to **Allah** by following his commandments, to freeing one from Shirk and the people of Shirk.

The Messenger of **Allah** (peace and blessings of **Allah** be upon him) said: "**Islam** is built on five (pillars): bearing witness that there is no deity worthy of worship except **Allah** and that **Muhammad** is the Messenger of **Allah**, establishing prayer, paying Zakah, Hajj and fasting Ramadan."

Islam is the religion of truth. I am a Muslim and I do not practice a religion other than Islam.

Allah the Most High said:

ومن يبتغ غير الاسلام دينا فلن يقبل منه وهو ـفي الاخرة من الخاسرين

Learn this Dua:

The Messenger of Allah ﷺ used to recite this Dua very often.

يا مقلب القلوب ثبت قلبي على دينك

Oh 'turner of the hearts'[**Allah**], keep my heart firm upon your religion (Islam).

The five pillars explained:

Shahadatain -To believe that Allah is the only one who should be worshipped in truth and Muhammad ﷺ is the messenger of Allah.

Salah-To pray five times a day.

Zakat-To give 2.5% charity on the value of your wealth.

Saum-To fast the Month of Ramadan.

Hajj-To perform Hajj to Makkah once in your lifetime.

Who taught us our religion, Islam?

Our Prophet **Muhammad Bin Abdullah bin Abdul Mutallib** ﷺ

Allah ﷻ sent him to the whole of mankind to invite them to the worship of the Creator[Allah] and not to worship any of the creation. So whoever obeyed him then he will enter the Paradise and whoever disobeyed him will enter the Hellfire.

I love my Prophet Muhammad ﷺ.

Muhammad ﷺ is the slave of Allah.

Muhammad ﷺ is the best of mankind.

Muhammad ﷺ is the Last Prophet of Allah; there is no Prophet after him.

Questions:

1. Who created the Sun, the Moon, the stars, the animals and humans?

   Answer...

2. Why did Allah create humans and Jinnkind?

   Answer...

3. Who sends down the rain from the sky?

   Answer...

4. Who is our Lord?

   Answer ....

5. Who is our Prophet?

   Answer ....

6. What is our religion?

Answer ....

7. Who do we make Dua to? Ask for help?

Answer ....

8. What are the 5 pillars of Islam?

Answer ....

....

9. What will happen to the earth if it does not rain?

Answer ....

10. How many branches of Tawheed?

Answer ....

Learn about Islam

Islam is my religion.

Islam means:

Islam is to submit to the will of **Allah** through **Tawheed**, then fully comply to **Allah** with obedience, and freeing one from Shirk and its people.

The word '**Islam**' indicates submission to **Allah** (Exalted be He), humbling oneself to Him, worshipping Him, and obeying His commands hence seeking the pleasure of **Allah**, who is your Lord. This is the essence of **Tawheed**, which is to be completely devoted and submitted to **Allah** (Exalted be He). The true Muslim, who understands **Tawheed**, is the one who submits himself to **Allah**, does his deeds purely for the sake of **Allah**, and directs his heart to **Allah** (Exalted be He) in secret and open, in fear and hope, in sayings, deeds, and totally depends on **Allah** for everything.

The proof is the saying of **Allah**, the Most Merciful:

إِنَّ الدِّينَ عِندَ اللَّهِ الْإِسْلَامُ

Indeed the religion with Allah is Islam. (Surah Aali Imran: 19)

Here Allah, the Most High is informing us that the only religion He will accept is Islam.

Complete the following sentences:

Islam is:

To Submit your will to the will of Allah with T_ _ _ _ _ d

To fully comply with the commands of Allah by total

Complete o _ _ _ _ _ n c e.

The Muslim should free himself from Shirk (making partners with Allah) and the people of S _ _ _ k.

The religion of truth: Islam

Islam is the religion of truth

Every other religion other than Islam is false.

I do not want a religion other than Islam. Islam is my religion.

The proof is the saying of Allah, the Truthful one:

وَمَن يَبْتَغِ غَيْرَ الْإِسْلَام دِينًا فَلَن يُقْبَلَ
مِنْهُ وَهُوَ فِي الْآخِرَةِ مِنَ الْخَاسِرِينَ

And whoever desires a religion other than Islam, it will never be accepted from him, and he, will be among the losers in the Hereafter. [Surah Al'Imran:85]

Learn this Dua:

يا مقلب القلوب ثبت قلبي على دينك

"'Oh turner of the hearts' [Allah], keep my heart firm on your religion (**Islam**)"

Narrated by Ahmed. The heart should always be busy with the remembrance of **Allah** so that the person feels happy and safe. The lips should also be moist with the remembrance of **Allah** in order to get close to **Allah** by doing good deeds.

Islam is built upon 5 pillars.

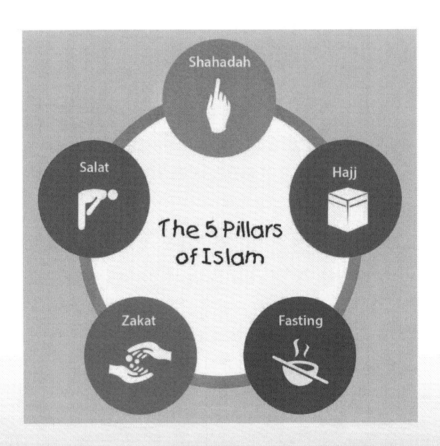

The first pillar is the most important pillar

then followed by the second pillar.

The proof is the saying of the Prophet ﷺ:

'**Islam** is built upon five [pillars]: testifying that there is none worthy of worship except **Allah** and that Muhammad is the Messenger of **Allah**, establishing the prayers, giving zakat, making the pilgrimage to the House and fasting the month of Ramadan.'" (Bukhari and Muslim).

Complete the following sentences:

The pillars of **Islam** are:

To testify that none has the right to be worshipped in truth except **Allah** and **Muhammad** is the Messenger of **Allah**.

Establishing the _____

Giving charity which is called _____

Making the pilgrimage to the House of **Allah**, in the city of Makkah al-Mukarramah, which is called _____

Fasting the month of

The Muslim should take care of these pillars, firstly have knowledge of them and then perform the actions. If the pillars are strong then Emaan is also strong.

A strong believer is the one who knows

his Tawheed, prays 5 times, pays Zakat, fasts in Ramadan and makes pilgrimage to Makkah.

Who taught us our religion, Islam?

Our Prophet **Muhammad Bin Abdullah bin Abdul Mutallib** ﷺ

Allah ﷻ sent him to the whole of mankind in order to call them to the worship of **Allah** alone and to leave the worship of others, besides **Allah**. So whoever obeyed him then he will enter the Paradise and whoever disobeyed him will enter the Hellfire.

I love my Prophet Muhammad ﷺ.

Muhammad ﷺ is the slave of Allah.

Muhammad ﷺ is the best of mankind.

Muhammad ﷺ is the Last Prophet of **Allah**; there is no Prophet after him.

Muhammad ﷺ is the slave of Allah and His

Messenger

My Prophet ﷺ is a slave of **Allah** from the slaves of **Allah**

The Proof is the saying of **Allah** ﷻ:

الْحَمْدُ لِلَّهِ الَّذِي أَنزَلَ عَلَى عَبْدِهِ الْكِتَابَ

All praise is due to Allah the one who sent down the Book (Quran) onto his slave. [Surah Al-Kahf: 1]

My Prophet **Muhammad** ﷺ is the best of mankind.

My Prophet **Muhammad** ﷺ is the Last of the Messengers sent by Allah.

The Proof is the saying of Allah:

وَلَكِن رَّسُولَ اللَّهِ وَخَاتَمَ النَّبِيِّينَ

But [he is] the Messenger of Allah and last of the prophets.[Surah Al-Ahzab: 40]

I say the following Zikr, three times every morning and evening.

رضيت بالله رباً وبالإسلام ديناً وبمحمدٍ رسولاً

I am pleased that Allah is the Lord; Islam is the religion and Muhammad in the Messenger.

Also, it is recommended to say this when the Muezzin (the one who calls the Adhan) says

أشهد أن لا إله إلا الله وأشهد أن محمدًا رسول الله

Which is the correct answer?

The first thing the Prophet **Muhammad** ﷺ called the people to:

Tawheed and warning against Shirk   o

Praying 5 times per day   o

Who is the best of mankind? _____

I love the Messenger of Allah ﷺ

I love my Prophet **Muhammad** ﷺ

I believe in the call of **Muhammad** ﷺ - everything he informed us through the Quran and the Sunnah is totally true.

I obey the Prophet ﷺ and do not disobey him.

Whoever obeys the Prophet ﷺ will enter paradise.

Allah the Most High said:

﴿وَمَن يُطِعِ اللَّهَ وَرَسُولَهُ يُدْخِلْهُ جَنَّاتٍ تَجْرِي مِن تَحْتِهَا الْأَنْهَارُ خَالِدِينَ فِيهَا وَذَلِكَ الْفَوْزُ الْعَظِيمُ﴾

Whoever obeys Allah and His Messenger will be admitted by Him to gardens [in Paradise] under which rivers flow, living there forever; and that is a great success.[Surah Al-Nisa: 13]

When the name of the Prophet **Muhammad** is mentioned then we say:

As-Salaah upon the Prophet is that Allah has mercy on the **Prophet** , the Angels make Dua for forgiveness and the people make Dua and also that a person asks Allah the Most High to aid the Deen of **Muhammad** , to mention and praise **Muhammad** in front of the angels in the heavens.

And "As-Salam" means to ask Allah to preserve him, preserve his Sunnah.

محمد رسول الله

This is Muhammad
Peace be upon him

Made in the USA
Columbia, SC
05 September 2023

22491388R00038